A Christian
View on
Relationships

A Christian View on Relationships

Mrs. Richardean Rosalind Gould-Meyers

ARPress
ILLUMINATING IDEAS
EMPOWERING VOICES

ARPress
45 Dan Road Suite 5
Canton MA 02021
Hotline: 1(888) 821-0229
Fax: 1(508) 545-7580

Ordering Information:
Quantity sales. Special discounts are available on quantity purchases by corporations, associations, and others. For details, contact the publisher at the address above.

Printed in the United States of America.

ISBN-13:	Softcover	979-8-89389-432-5
	eBook	979-8-89389-433-2

Library of Congress Control Number: 2024917789

Table of Contents

INTRODUCTION

I have finished writing my book with the help of the Lord. The Enemy will try to steal your purpose. Now God is inspiring me to write another book. My book is called A Christian View on relationships. The core of the matter is that the enemy dwells in the supernatural. He bounces back and forth in the spiritual realms he causes chaos everywhere he goes. His focus is on every aspect of our lives and especially our relationships as well. His focus is to bring us down in every aspect of our lives, he tries to break us. Yes, we are human beings. Yes, we are responsible for our own actions, yes, we are but the root of our suffering is the enemy, yes, it is. The Lord knows that the devil has put a lot of obstacles in front of me and my husband and thank the Lord we are still standing Amen.

You always want somebody in your corner if you are injured and you cannot take yourself to your doctor's appointment. They'll be right there by your side every step of the way, so you won't miss any of your doctor's appointments. God Bless. Thank You, Honey. I love this journey that God has me on now. I hope this book will bless each and every one of you and let you see the root of the matter in your relationship. If you're having any problems that the enemy, he is somewhere around the corner causing chaos for you. Sometimes it can be in the natural but most of the time it's in the supernatural.

We have to start paying close attention to our surroundings and situations that occur in our lives because we don't want the enemy to take advantage of us; we don't want the enemy to use us for his personal gain. The enemy loves splitting couples up. The enemy wants us broken in every aspect of our lives. He tries to hit us hard. He loves hitting us in our relationship. He wants us to suffer. The enemy wants you to have no joy

or happiness in your life. So, he hits us hard in our relationships. Making us suffer makes us feel bad about ourselves, making us fight one another. He is a black cloud over us. We need to draw closer to God so God can instruct us on how to bring the enemy down. He is trying to destroy your well-being so pay close attention and always pray for yourself and your families and your fellowman, Amen.

I thank God for allowing me to take this journey again and to write this book. I hope this book will touch your lives in a positive way and bring joy to your lives. I thank Father God for the Family that I have and allowing them to come on this journey with me again as well. God is my strength, and through my relationship with God, I'm able to do all things, Amen. I pray that my book will inspire you and change your lives for the better. May God be with you all.

CHAPTER 1

AT THE BEGINNING OF CREATION OF MAN AND WOMAN.

GENESIS 1,1-31 2,1-25

At first, God made the heavens and the earth. And the earth was wasteful and without form and it was dark on the face of the deep and the spirit of God was moving on the face of the waters.

And God said, Let there be light and there was light. And God looking on the light saw that it was good, and God made a division between the light and the dark, Naming the light, Day, and the darkness Night. And there was evening and there was morning, the first day.

And God said, Let there be a solid arch stretching over the waters, parting the waters from the waters. And God made the arch for a division between the waters which were under the arch and those which were over it and it was so. And God gave the arch the name of Heaven. And there was evening and there was morning, the second day.

And God said, Let the waters under the heavens come together in one place, and let the dry land be seen and it was so. And God gave the dry land the name of the earth; and the waters together in their place were named Seas and God saw that it was good.

And God said, Let grass come upon the earth, and plants produce seeds, after their sort and it was so. And grass came upon the earth, and every plant producing seeds of its sort, and every tree producing fruit, in

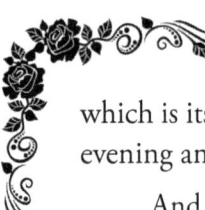

which is its seed, of its sort and God saw that it was good. And there was evening and there was morning, the third day.

And God said, Let there be lights in the arch of Heaven for a division between the day and the night, and let them be for signs, and for marking the changes of the year, and for days and for years. And let them be for lights in the arch of heaven to give light on the earth and it was so. And God made two great lights, the greater light to be the ruler of the day, and the smaller light to be the ruler of the night and he made the stars. And God put them in the arch of Heaven, to give light on the earth. To have the rule over the day and the night, and for a division between the light and the dark, and God saw that it was good. And there was evening and there was morning, the fourth day.

And God said, Let the waters be full of living things, and let birds in flight over the earth under the arch of Heaven. And God made great sea-beasts, and every sort of living and moving thing with which the waters were full, and every sort of winged bird and God saw that it was good. And God gave them his blessing, saying, be fertile and have increased, making all the waters of the seas full, and let the birds be increased in the earth. And there was evening and there was morning, the fifth day.

And God said, Let the earth give birth to all sorts of living things, cattle and all things moving on the earth, and beasts of the earth after their sort and it was so. And God made the beast of the earth after its sort, and everything moved on the face of the earth after its sort and God saw that it was good.

And God said, Let us make man in our image, like us and let him have the rule over the fish of the sea and over the birds of the air and over the cattle and over all the earth and over every living thing which goes flat on the earth.

And God made man in his image, in the image of God, he made him make male and female he made them.

And God gave them his blessing and said to them, Be fertile and have increased, and made the earth full and be masters of it, be rulers over the fish of the sea and over the birds of the air and over every living thing moving on the earth. And God said, see I have given you every plant producing seed, on the face of all the earth, and every tree that has

fruit producing seed they will be for your food. And to every beast of the earth and to every bird of the air and every living thing moving on the face of the earth I have given every green plant for food, and it was so. And God saw everything which he had made, and it was very good. And there was evening and there was morning, the sixth day.

And the heavens and the earth and all things in them were complete. And on the seventh day God came to the end of all his work and on the seventh day he took his rest from all work which he had done. And God gave his blessing to the seventh day and made Holy because on that day took his rest from all the work which he had made and done.

These are the generations of the heavens and the earth when they were made. On the day when the Lord God made the earth and the heavens there were no plants of the field on the earth and no grass had come up for the Lord God had not sent rain on the earth and there is no man to do work on the land. But a mist went up from the earth, watering all the face of the land.

And the Lord God made man from the dust of the earth breathing into him the breath of life and man because a living soul. And the Lord God made a garden in the east, in Eden and there he put the man whom he had made. And out of the earth the Lord made every tree to come, delighting the eye and good for food and in the middle of the garden the tree of life and the tree of the knowledge of good and evil.

And a river went out of Eden watering the garden, and from there it parted and became four streams. The name of the first is Pishon, which goes round about all the land Havilah where there is gold. And the gold of that land is good there is bdellium and the onyx stone. And the name of the second river is Gihon. This river goes round all the land of Cush. And the name of the third river is Tigris which goes to the east of Assyria. And the fourth river is the Euphrates.

And the Lord God took the man and put him in the garden of Eden to work it and take care of it. And the Lord God gave the man orders, saying, You may freely take of the fruit of every tree of the garden. But of the fruit of the tree of the knowledge of good and evil you may not take for on the day when you take it, death will certainly come to you.

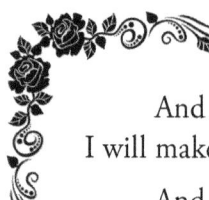

And the Lord God said it is not good for the man to be by himself. I will make one like himself as a help to him.

And from the earth the Lord God made every beast of the field and every bird of the air and took them to the man to see what names he would give them whatever name he gave to any living thing, that was its name. And the man gave names to all cattle and to the birds of the air and to every beast of the field, but Adam had no one like himself as a help. And the Lord God sent deep sleep on the man and took one of the bones from his side while he was sleeping, joining up the flesh again in its place. And the bone which the Lord God had taken from the man he made into a woman and took her to the man.

And the man said, This is now bone of my bone and flesh of my flesh. Let her name be Woman because she was taken out of man.

For this, his father and his mother will be joined to his wife, and they will be one flesh. And the man and his wife were without clothing, and they had no sense of shame.

You can see right in GENESIS that God's intent is for us not to be alone. Adam and Eve were the first married couple. In an appropriate time, God took Eve to Adam. My understanding from that is that God wants us to wait until he gives us our mate. That's what I can see in that scripture. Adam was alone and then God gave him Eve. What it looks like to me if you wait patiently for your mate Father God will give him or her to you. I think if we pray and become one with the Father things will be better for us. And receive Jesus Christ in our lives. The reason why I said that is because in the beginning we were one with the Father before the devil destroyed that for us so now, we have to go through this whole process to become one with God again. God loves us, there's nothing on this earth that he would not do for us. He wants us to be happy. God does not want us feeling bad inside suffering. He wants you whole in every aspect of your life before you start stepping into the realm of dating. You should wait for the Lord patiently. Adam did God give him Eve, yes, at the beginning they had a little hiccup. Through it all God bless them with children Cain and Abel and Seth. Through all that drama that the devil put them through their relationship remains strong in the lord. Amen.

CHAPTER 2

Adam

In the beginning, God created Adam, and right from the start, God had a relationship in mind for him. This is my take on the matter; God wants you to be whole in every aspect of your life. God designed us; He has the floor plan. He is the creator of the universe. God is the core, the root of our solution; He has the answers. We need to follow him, and He will give us the answers to our problems.

This means in the beginning, God wanted Adam to experience joy and happiness in his life, that's why he gave him Eve. God wants us to experience that same joy and happiness as well. God wants you to be complete in every aspect of your life before you step forward into the realm of dating, as dating is serious business. We do not have all the answers; God has all the answers. God did not intend for us to suffer when it comes to relationships. God's intent was for us to be one with him and happy. Amen, Amen.

My take on this matter is that God waited for Adam to be one hundred percent whole in every aspect of his life before he introduced him to Eve. God wants you to be complete in your heart, your soul, your spirit, your mind, before God introduces you to your soulmate. Amen. God Bless You.

CHAPTER 3

Eve

The enemy could see right from the beginning that Eve was getting ready to receive happily ever after. The devil, having destroyed his own relationship with God, now plans to destroy our lives as well. We are one with Eve; we are connected to Eve. So, what happened to her in the garden, we are experiencing right now, just like it happened to us. Because we are twinned with her, we share that moment in time with her when the devil deceived her.

That's why Jesus died on the cross-so we can have a second chance at life, from that mistake in the path. God's intent was for us to be happy in a relationship. That was God's intent. God did not intend for us to suffer in relationships. God gave Eve joy and happiness right from the start, but the devil was right there on the scene, trying to take it from her. At that moment in time before the devil stepped in and destroyed Adam and Eve happiness. They did have that happily ever after that God intended for us to have.

That happily ever after God intended for relationships to work. God made humankind for us to be together in harmony as one. God loves family. In the beginning of Genesis, he told us to go and multiply and be fertile. You can't be fertile by yourself; you need two people to be fertile. So, God intended right there from the start for man and woman to be together as one, in a relationship. However, that was not the enemy intent; right there on the spot, he brought confusion, and he separated the man from the woman. We need to pay close attention to that.

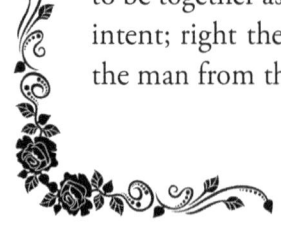

God wants us to have love, peace and togetherness. The enemy does not want us to have love, peace and togetherness. Togetherness is the key. Amen.

CHAPTER 4

Prayer is powerful

Dating is serious business because when you start dating, you have to put yourself out there, because you are looking for someone to spend your time with or you're looking for someone to spend the rest of your life with. Before you start doing that, make sure you get on your hands and knees and pray to God. Ask God to come into the room to cover you on this journey, that you are about to take in the dating realm. Because you are going to be interacting with a lot of different people and a lot of different spirits, so you want to be covered when you're interacting with these people.

Pray on this journey–prayer is powerful. Pay attention to your surroundings. Pay attention to the people that you are interacting with. Make sure your spirit and their spirit connect, if your spirit and their spirit don't connect, then he or she is not the one. When you meet a person, you want your spirit and their spirit to connect. You can feel your spirit together. It's deep. If you meet someone at the beginning and your spirit and their spirit don't mix, be careful dating the person, because you don't want to be in any drama in the long run. Because one thing about the enemy is he will mix you up with people that's not compatible for you to put you in some drama.

You want to have peace of mind on this journey of dating and good experience. Make sure you continue to pray on this journey, because God will let you know when your soulmate comes, because he will bring them to you. Amen.

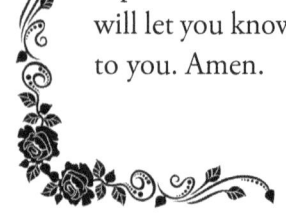

CHAPTER 5

God is love

God is love. God is nothing but love. He is always there for us. He wants you to be happy. Amen. Be careful out there when you're dating, and make sure that you and the person click. Sometimes the devil will make you think that you and the person like each other when it's not so, and later down the line, the devil will have you caught up in a lot of drama. You don't want drama in your life, you want nothing but positivity flowing your way. You want dating to be a wonderful experience for you, you don't want the devil to mess it up for you. Amen.

So always put God first in your life so he can cover you through your journey in life. Always ask God for his advice before you step out and do anything in life. Always pray, always have that mindset to have God on your mind one hundred percent every single day. Amen.

Remember that the enemy is real and remember that he is the cause of a lot of drama in your life and the negative force that comes upon you in your life. That's him so, be careful. Some people say that the enemy doesn't bother your relationship. I say that's not true because the enemy has been messing with our relationship since the beginning of time he has been. Remember, now he was in the garden of Eden trying to put a wedge between Adam and Eve, God. God Bless. Love You All.

CHAPTER 6

Prayer Changes Things

Prayer changes things. Prayer is the solution to our problems. We need prayer because we cannot do anything without Father God on our side, one hundred percent, every single day. With the enemy running rapidly in our lives today, we need to stay on our hands and knees, praying at all times. Amen.

We have to start paying close attention to our surroundings and situations that occur in our lives. Because we don't want the devil to take advantage of us. We don't want the devil to use us for his personal gain. We do not want him to use us-not one bit. So, get behind us, Satan and hear us roar; you're not going to mess with us anymore, because we have the power to take you down. We have Father God on our side, seven days of week. Amen.

Father God will give you the tools that you need. Receive Jesus Christ in your life, and He will be there for you forever. Amen. God Bless.

CHAPTER 7

The enemy likes to split up relationships with your family members as well

The enemy likes to split up relationships with your family members as well. I have noticed that, at this moment in time in our lives, the enemy has all of our family members fighting each other for no reason whatsoever. It goes back to the beginning when the devil spilled all his negativity out here in the atmosphere, trying to get us to destroy ourselves.

We need prayer; we need to pray as we never prayed before. Because the enemy is trying to destroy all of our lives by hitting us in our relationships as well. The core of the matter is negativity. If you see negativity around, then that's him. For no reason at all, your family members start saying something negative to you for no reason whatsoever. Believe me, that's him--he's responsible for all the negativity that's here in the world today and then some. He tries to play around with your feelings. That is the key he likes to manipulate things.

Be careful and be aware of this. Pray for your family members all the time, and always has Christ on your mind because you're going to need Christ to cover you in all the certain situations that are coming up in your life today. The enemy is a spirit that moves around in realms. He causes chaos everywhere he goes. The enemy despises happiness and relationships.

Let me give you an example; You and your family members are having a cookout, everyone is having a wonderful time. No one is upset

with no one, everyone is happy. All of a sudden one of your family members says something inappropriate to another family member. For no reason whatsoever, now all the family members are arguing with each other. However, what had happened is that the enemy was walking by and saw that you were happy. Happiness is the key and infects one of your family members with negativity. Because the family members were happy the enemy did not like people showing signs of affection between each other.

Sometimes, you can feel that burning sensation inside of you, that you are getting ready to get upset. So, take that as a sign that the enemy is trying to destroy your happiness. Fight that sensation and continue on with your family members and have a lovely day with them. Don't let the enemy win in your life.

Family is the key family; that it makes the world go around. You shouldn't be separated from your family. You and your family should always be in one realm together. Don't let the enemy split your family apart, if you are engaging in a conversation with your family member, and all at once you start to get angry with your family member for no reason. Take a breath, walk away, pray, try to hold yourself together, don't let the enemy win. After you have calmed yourself down, then go back to your family member and say I'm sorry. I don't know what came over me, but I love you. Let's start this conversation again, don't let the enemy win.

CHAPTER 8

Relationships

In a relationship, you can be sweet and kind, nice or not. Sometimes someone might say, "But I do give physical things I'm always giving. I don't know what this person wants from me. I treat him or her well." Sometimes, people are not aware of their behavior. They think by taking you somewhere, giving you gifts, they excuse the behavior that they have towards you.

When someone is being hostile towards you, talking to you in a manner that you will not talk to your father or your mother too, do you honestly think that this person is going to submit to you, even listen to you, you are making this person become numb towards you? It's all about your tone towards someone-- that is the key. If you talk sweet and kind to someone, they will give you the world. If you are talking to someone in an aggressive manner on a day-to-day basis, believe me, brothers and sisters, they are going to start shutting down and you're not going to like what you see in this person's attitude towards you.

Think about this behavior honestly, to God. Would you want someone to treat you like this?

CHAPTER 9

Break- up

There are different stages of a break-up. But one thing about all the stages, is that it will stop you in the core of your universe, especially when it was unexpected. Especially when you thought that you were going to spend the rest of your life with that person.

When the person is telling you that they're breaking up with you and they're giving you their reason, you are standing there, listening to what they are saying to you in disbelief because you cannot believe what you are hearing from this person's mouth. At that moment in time, what's running in your head is like, "Oh my God, I thought that this person loved me. I thought that our love was special. I cannot believe this person is doing me like this. What is wrong with this person? Oh my God."

Usually at that moment in time, two scenarios will take place. Scenarios one; you will leave the relationship gracefully, and you will remain the same--your heart, your soul, your spirit, your mind will remain the same. You will be the same person that you were at that moment in time that the person was breaking up with you. That incident didn't affect you one bit--you remain the same. Amen.

Scenario two; you cannot believe what this person is saying to you. They are crushing your heart, your soul, your spirit, your mind. What's going on in your mind at that moment in time is that you thought that this person was your soulmate, and you were meant for each other. So now you are stuck at that moment in time, reliving that moment when the person breaks up with you over and over in your head.

At that moment in time, you are feeling like all your trials and tribulations are coming upon you at one moment. But if you reach your hands up to the sky and call on Jesus, he will give you the knowledge to get you some help. God will encourage you to reach out to a Christian counselor or a counselor or someone you know to talk to. Sometimes we pray and we pray for God to help us, but sometimes when a burden is so heavy on your heart like this, it's all right to step out in faith and talk to someone because God does not want us to suffer.

God loves us all. God wants us to have a wonderful life. But the devil is somewhere in the mix of the situation destroying our lives. Pray to God, and if you're in a situation like this, reach out for help. God is always with you. God Bless Love You All. Sometimes God comes in the form of a person. Amen.

CHAPTER 10

Heartbreak

Sometimes, after a break-up, you're going through some struggles in life. Just keep praying to God and keep pushing through. God is there for you. God loves you, He's always there for you. Amen.

Sometimes, your heart feels like it's breaking into two pieces literally. Just stay focused on the Lord because, in a situation like this, you just need to draw closer and closer to God, because God is the one that's going to bring you through this drama that the enemy put upon you.

Anything negatives that comes against you in your life, believe me, it's the enemy. The enemy is the one out there pouring all the negativity into the world. So, if you experience negativity in your life, it's the enemy. Be aware of your surroundings, and always know what's going on. God bless you.

CHAPTER 11

After a break-up and Heartbreak don't step into another relationship so soon

When you are just coming out of a breakup, you need to take your time. Before you get back out there and start dating, you need to relax. Your spirit, your soul, your heart, and your mind need clarity. Amen.

Because your soul just took a shaking, it just went through some trauma. You need to relax and get yourself back together again. Amen. Pray for every aspect of your life; pray for it. Your heart has been broken, so you have to work on mending it back together. Amen.

Your mental state is a very important first step in getting yourself back together. Having a deep relationship with God is the one thing that is going to pull you through this situation that you're in. God didn't intend for you to be having it rough in these relationships; God intended for you to have peace of mind. Pray to God, eventually, he will turn this situation around and have faith.

It's okay to speak to a Christian counselor; they are a blessing from God. You will want to get back to yourself again. If you have children, focus on them. That is a big help. If you have a job, you need to pour yourself into that job. You need to keep your mind positive and busy. You don't want your mind going back to that negative moment in your life, you want to keep a positive frame of mind. Amen. Stay positive; God Is with You.

CHAPTER 12

Marriage

Marriage is sacred. God has blessed two people together forever. Amen. No one should come between two married people. God connected them together forever. You should not try to put a wedge between them.

If someone is married, why would you be in their faces acting like they are single, and you know that they are married? People have no respect for the sacredness of marriage today. Yes, God sees all. God thinks highly of marriage. We have no respect for our fellow man today; what we want is what we want, and we want it now, and we do not care about who we knocked down and walk over to get it.

We should all respect marriage because it's sacred. God is in the mix of marriage. God believes in marriage, so when you get married, you should take it seriously. Because it is no joke to be married. If you are playing around with the person that you are getting ready to marry, and you're not serious about marriage, then don't marry the person. You do not want to get married and then go down the line, and you and the person break up.

Marriage is serious business. You are splitting the family in half; most of the time, the children suffer. Because you are not truly serious about the moment, you're just in the moment and you haven't really thought about it. Before you step into the realm of marriage, be counseled by a Christian Council or someone that can help you through

the process because marriage is serious, and it is sacred. You shouldn't play with marriage, because it is too much involved in marriage.

If you just want to play around with someone. Then you play around with someone, but don't step over into the realm of marriage. Prayer works if you work it. God listens to prayer if you want to marry someone you need to take it to God. God is the only one who can see if you and that person are the right person for each other. Because you don't want to walk into the realm of marriage just for a couple of days. You want to be in a marriage for the long run.

Marriage is serious business, so if you don't think that you can be in a marriage for a long run, then don't step in that realm. There's a lot of people involved when you marry, one person when you have children. That's another realm to pray hard for before you step into the realm of marriage.

God bless you. I am not passing judgment on anyone; I just don't want anyone in unnecessary pain. And I am not saying that people should fool around with each other. What I am saying is if you are not serious about someone and you do not think that you can commit to that person, then don't marry that person. Don't draw that person into your drama. That's all I'm saying. God bless you all.

CHAPTER 13

Divorce Is Hard

Divorce can be hard on someone's spirit and life, thinking in their mind that they are a failure because they're divorced. God loves us all. Keep on pushing and pushing through. Don't let this moment in time define who you are one bit.

We have gone through storms in our lives, and at that moment in time, it looks hopeless. God has always pulled us through to the other side, where there is nothing but rainbows all around us. Always think about God; always have God in your heart. God loves you and God is the root of your solution. He will always be there for you. Amen.

So don't ever think that you are a failure--you are not a failure. You were born from greatness. So, hold your head up high; you are one of God's chosen people. God has chosen you for something great. Don't let any negative moment in your life define who you are--you know who you are.

Sometimes, people are caught up in a moment in time, that they think that the person that they are getting ready to marry is their soulmate. The enemy manipulates the situation so you and the person you are marrying think it's true love. The enemy has tricked you in this marriage to cause you to get a divorce.

The enemy does not like married couples. The enemy does not like couples at all. The enemy's assignment is to try to destroy our well-being. So, don't worry. Hold your head up high and keep moving towards the light. Jesus is the light. One day, God will give you your true soulmate. Everyone has one--you just have to wait patiently for him or her from God. Amen.

CHAPTER 14

When you find your Love

When you find your true love and you know that they are the one for you. Hold on to them for dear life, and don't let anyone try to tell you--that they are not the one for you. Amen. If you know that this person is your soulmate and you know that he or she is your love, don't let anyone tell you anything different. You do not know the person's motives.

The enemy is the root of your problems, especially when you are happy. He does not want you to be happy so, He focuses on you. And when he sees that you are very happy, then he strikes hard. Sometimes it's him in the form of a person, or he is using one of his minions he is using for his negativity against you. Amen.

If you focus and you take a good look, you will see that every aspect of your life is under attack by the enemy. So always focus on the positive so when negativity comes against you, you can know the difference and you can know that something is not right in the atmosphere. Don't ever let anyone take your joy and happiness away from you. Always stay positive, always focus on the positive realm of life. God Bless, love You All.

Be careful who you listen to about your relationship, because sometimes people don't have your best interest at heart. Sometimes their motive is not pure so always pay attention to your surroundings. And when you are under attack by the enemy God will fight your battles for you. Yes, he will.

CHAPTER 15

Running Around

When someone is being dishonest in a relationship, they're running around sneaking with someone, is that appropriate behavior? They're sneaking around in the dark, and this person will never bring you to the light. What do you think about that behavior? Your boyfriend or your girlfriend will not introduce you to their mom, dad or anyone in their family. So, you're running around with this person, thinking you're having a relationship with them. You know that this person is involved with someone else, but you don't care--you just want what you want.

Usually when you are running around, that behavior is temporary. You are in a delusional state at that moment in time, but it's not real. When you look up at that moment, you have lost everything you have. Your husband is leaving, you or your wife is leaving you. Someone is leaving you.

When you are running around, at that moment, you feel fantastic. You feel awesome. But that state that you're in is a delusional state of mind. It's not real--it's just temporary. It's going to fade away. At some point, you will come back to your senses, and you have lost everything. Amen.

Think about what you are doing. Think and say to yourself. "Would Jesus be doing this? Am I acting Christ-like? Am I proud of myself at this time?" If you are causing someone grief and suffering intentionally, what you put in the atmosphere, you will receive it back in your life, whether good or bad. That is the way the system is designed- what you put in the atmosphere you will receive it back in your life. Amen. Someone will treat you like this one day.

CHAPTER 16

Betrayal

Betrayal is very devastating to the soul. Amen. It'll stop you right there in your tracks. You will feel like you are falling in the pit of hell, and only Father God himself can reach down there in the pit of hell and pull you out. Amen. That's how you feel when someone betrays you, and then you feel more than that as well. Your soul has been taken to a place that you have never been to before.

If you are not religious, by the time you are done with this process--with the emotions going back and forth, your good days and bad days--I know when you're going through this situation, you're going to need to hold on to someone. I believe in that moment; you are going to call on Jesus. You are going to ask Jesus to step in and take away this pain because this pain that I am going through is unbearable for me to handle. "Help me Jesus, help me". Amen.

When someone you love betrays you, it will shake the core of your universe. You are in total shock and disbelief. You don't know what to do at that moment. You are going to need Jesus Christ himself to pull you through this trauma. When you are going through this trauma that has been placed upon your soul, and if someone appears at your house to talk to you, sometimes it's okay to talk to someone. Because sometimes God sends people on his behalf to talk to you, you will no. So you can release some of that burden off of your shoulder due to that trauma that you are going through at that moment in time. Amen.

Always pray. Always have that mindset to have Jesus Christ on your mind. Always pray because prayer is definitely the key to getting you through. Amen.

May God Bless You.

CHAPTER 17

Have compassion toward your fellowman

Put Father God first in every aspect of your life. Always pray for your family, always put your family ahead of yourself. Always pray for your fellowman, always have compassion toward your fellowman, always bless your fellowman if it's possible--always try. God always wants you to look out for your fellowman of course.

Always pray for yourself, because your family needs you as well as always do that. Please, God loves us all. God wants us to show compassion toward each other. Amen.

And try to stay in a positive mind frame. Try to bring some joy and happiness into someone's life. Don't complain because once you start complaining, you open the door for negativity to walk right in. Always pray, always think positive, always stay positive, always be positive. God is looking down at us and he wants us to do our best. Amen.

May God Bless you.

CHAPTER 18

People are looking for real love

People are looking for real love that connects, that spark. Amen. That real love--someone to really love, not playing games with them. Not toying with their feelings. Amen.

God has designed someone special for each one of us. When God designed us, He had a suitable mate in mind. When he designed us, he did not design us to be in a relationship with someone that might be playing games with us. They're not really there to spend time with you; they're there to get what they want from you.

Just pray to God and make sure, before you put your whole self into a relationship, pray and see if this really the person for you. Is this the man or the woman God really intended me to be with? Pray for that. I want everybody to be on the right track in life. Amen. Because love does exist.

May God Bless You All.

CHAPTER 19

When someone dumps you

When someone dumps you, I know it can be devastating. But we need to move past that moment in time. We cannot allow that negative moment that happened to us to define who we are right now. We have to rise up in our spirit; we cannot let that moment paralyze us and let it keep repeating that moment.

We have to move past that moment. We cannot let the devil win in our lives anymore. We have to take back our lives from him. Amen. God has given us this life. I will rise up from that moment in time; I will not let the enemy destroy my life. We are going to continue to push through and continue to pray because there is always a silver lining after all that drama that the devil has put you through.

God loves you. He does not want you walking around suffering; He wants you to live your life to the fullest. Amen. May God Bless You All.

CHAPTER 20

Soulmate

Everyone prays to have a soulmate. Somebody that they are one hundred percent connected to when they meet for the first time, when they look into each other's eyes. They have a connection to this person like they never had before. Amen. And you know in your spirit that this person is the one for you. Amen. Soulmates do exist, really. God has given you this joy in your life, and you don't want to lose this experience in life. God wants us to be happy; He wants that joy in our lives. The enemy is the one that does not want joy and happiness in our lives.

The enemy will set you up with people in your life to destroy your wellbeing, to aggravate you, to stress you out. When you are looking for your soulmate or someone to date, don't be concerned about how the person looks. Don't focus on the physical; focus on the spiritual focus on how the person's energy and how is the person's spirit. When you are next to the person, notice how you feel from their energy. Amen. Your energy and spirit are connected together, so if you're standing next to someone, you can feel their energy. You can feel their spirit and you can feel a connection or not.

Pay attention to that. Pay attention to all of that, please. Pay attention when you first meet the person. Do you feel a connection? Do you feel chemistry between you and the person? Pay attention to all of that, stay in a positive mind frame when you're doing all that. Pay attention. You do not want to be caught up in the drama. You're looking for your soulmate. You are not looking for the enemy. You don't want to

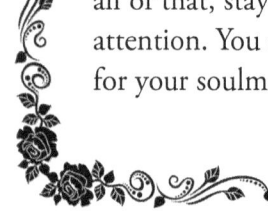

start dating the enemy, because once you start dating the enemy, he has you caught up in all this drama. You thought that he or she was a good person and in reality, he or she was not a good person. He or she was the enemy. But the person was wrapped up in a package looking like he or she was a good person. But he or she is not.

So, that's why you have to pay close attention to your surroundings. Pay close attention. To your energy and spirit. If this person's energy doesn't connect with you, you know that this is not the one. God does not want you caught up in the drama. God wants nothing but positivity flowing your way. Pay Close Attention. Amen.

CHAPTER 21

Bringing baggage from one relationship to another

When you have had a bad break-up or you left the relationship in a negative way, before you step into another relationship, relax – take your time, and don't rush into another relationship so quickly. You don't want to take the negativity from the old relationship into your new relationship. You don't want to bring that old baggage into your new relationship.

What is going to happen is the negativity that will affect your new relationship. You don't want to bring that old baggage with you, you are going to be thinking about the path you might have flashbacks, and the current person will be the target, but you are not really targeting the current person; it is really towards your ex. So, relax your spirit, your mind, your soul, and pray a lot.

Just don't step into another relationship so quickly. Think about it, get all that negativity out of your system, put positivity into your system so that when you step into a new relationship, things will be great. Everything will be roses, and you won't be having flashbacks about your ex. It'll be all about the current person. Amen.

When something like that happens to you, it puts you in a negative State of Mind. You want to get back to your positive State of Mind and want to get away from the negativity that cripples your spirit. May God bless everyone.

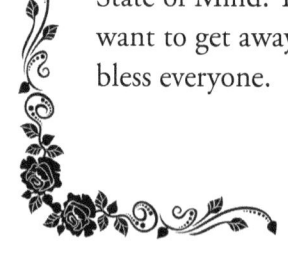

CHAPTER 22

A person that just cannot commit

Sometimes, a person cannot commit to you because they might have been hurt in the past. They could feel that if they give you their whole heart and soul, you will do the same thing to them. What the other person did to them. So that's why they won't open up to you. That's why they are so guarded.

Sometimes in a relationship, things happen to people at that moment in time, and it affects them for their whole life. It can be very devastating to someone. God did not intend for us to suffer in a relationship; that was not his intent. God's plan was for us not to be alone. My take on that. means that he wants us to be a couple. He wants us to be in a relationship with someone. That means that it is a blessing to be in a relationship with someone. It is truly a blessing from God.

So, God did not design a relationship for us to be in with people and we are suffering in the relationship. A relationship is something sacred, something holy that God has made he's brought us together as one. Amen. Do you honest-to-God think that God approves of people in relationships hurting each other? Playing games with each other, treating them very badly, dismissing them, not paying them any mind whatsoever--do you think that is God's intention? No, that's not God's intent.

God wants us to find someone that is compatible for us, to love us, and adore us, and we come together as one in Christ. Amen. That's God's intent. God loves us dearly. When He brings us together with

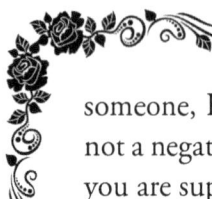 

someone, He is bringing us together with this person in a positive way, not a negative way. Because when you are in a relationship with someone, you are supposed to love that person, be kind and sweet, and treat them like they are the only person that matters in the world to you. Amen.

P.S. When it comes to relationships we are losing the war, people are just afraid to get out there anymore, they don't want to get hurt. May God bless them, God give them the strength to keep going. Amen.

CHAPTER 23

You should not force your beliefs on someone

You should not force your beliefs on someone when you are dating. If you like to date multiple people, you need to tell them that right at the beginning. Sometimes, people like to be in a relationship with just one person, Amen. If you believe in dating multiple people, that's fine, and that's dandy because that's your belief. But sometimes, people believe in just dating one person at a time.

So, at the beginning, if you tell the person that you are seeing multiple people at the same time, you give that person a chance to say, "I don't want to see you anymore" or, "Okay, that's fine and dandy with me. I date multiple people as well" Or, they'll tell you, "I'm sorry. I'm just a person to date, one person, at a time." You give the person the choice to be in a relationship with you, and don't force your beliefs on them. Amen.

When you are being deceitful, you are opening the door for the evil one to walk in. He dwells in negativity, so if you are being dishonest, that's where he dwells. You don't want him destroying your happiness because you are being deceitful. Always be honest, and the evil one won't be lurking around your corner.

When people are looking for love, they're not looking for people to be deceiving them – they're looking for honest people to love them. Amen.

CHAPTER 24

The enemy likes to break-up people's relationships

The enemy likes to break up people's relationships. I believe if we all get on one accord and be nice, kind and sweet to one another, then we won't give the enemy any ammunition to target our relationship. Because once the enemy sees something negative in your relationship, that's where he focuses on it. He dwells in negativity.

God is positivity; God dwells in positivity–nothing but positivity, Amen, Amen. If we stay positive, have a positive start of mind, and don't allow negativity to affect us, then we don't give the enemy any ammunition towards us. He only targets us when he sees something negative going on. So, if we stay positive and do positive things, then he can't focus on us.

If the enemy is walking by and he sees a crowd of happy people, he will Target the one that's being sinful. So don't give him an opportunity to target you–always walk in righteousness. Amen. May God Bless You All.

CHAPTER 25

The enemy will try to destroy your well-being

In the beginning, the enemy came after Eve and tried to destroy her family. Now, he is after us as well. The enemy has unleashed all this negativity into the atmosphere, and we are affected by it. We are breathing in his negativity on a day-to-day basis, and the enemy is happy because he loves the negativity to grow. You can see in the atmosphere today how this world is being affected by the negativity that the enemy is breathing into this world today.

We need Jesus like we never needed Him before. The enemy hits you in every aspect of your life; he's coming for every aspect. In the beginning, you can see that he was trying to destroy the family and the relationship. If you pay close attention, you can see that he tried to divide the family, and he tried to divide couples. He does not want unity, so he will throw a wedge right there in your family so you and your family can bicker back and forth, and you can have a cloud of despair over your head, and he is happy with that.

We need to stand up on one accord and fight a good fight of faith. With Jesus on our side, we cannot lose. We do not want the enemy to win, not one bit in our lives today. Pray, and pray as you've never prayed before, and take the necessary steps to receive Jesus Christ in your life. Amen. May God Bless You.

CHAPTER 26

Forgiveness

When you forgive someone, truly forgive them. Pray on the matter and let it go. Don't keep dwelling on it, and don't keep throwing it up in the person's face. When you forgive someone, you truly forgive them—you let it go. God will receive that issue, He will take care of it, He will give you the strength to really forgive a person, and He will give you peace inside of your spirit. So, let it go and give it to God, and he will give you peace of mind. Amen.

God loves us all, there's nothing in this world that He would not do for us. His love is everlasting. Amen. God bless—stay positive. Always keep Father God strong in your heart. He is always there for you, and He will always have your back one hundred percent every day. Amen.

Real forgiveness when you tell someone. "I forgive you," you might think about what they did to you now and then, but you won't bring it up to them. Because you have been raised above that, and you would let that situation go, and you would never bring it up again. God has sealed that moment in time for you, and He has helped you through it—that is true forgiveness. Amen.

God Bless You.

CHAPTER 27

Sometimes it's hard to move on

Sometimes, it's hard to move on from a break-up. Sometimes the person might sit there and wonder if the person is coming back to them, and they won't move past that moment. Sometimes they just sit there, and they won't leave the house, just wondering and wandering, and they're stuck in time at that moment when the person left them.

Usually, at that moment in time, if you're not religious, you usually draw closer to God. You try to find some kind of relationship with Him because you're trying to find some meaning about what's going on with you. Amen.

Sometimes, it's good to draw closer to your family. Yes, the family can be your rock. Your family can push you through that moment in time by keeping you happy by encouraging you in a positive way. They can be your medicine. Always pray and stay positive. Amen.

CHAPTER 28

God loves us and he wants us to be happy

God loves us. He truly loves us. God wants us to be one hundred percent happy in every aspect of our lives. He does not want us to suffer, not one bit. Amen. So, when we are going through these trials and tribulations, he's right there by our side every step of the way encouraging us.

We love the Lord, yes, we do. We might have situations in life, but God will always be there for us. So always give God the glory; He is worthy to be praised. Without him in our lives, we cannot do anything. Honest to God, I know I can't do anything without His divine help. Amen.

And always embrace your family. Always have your family around you because your family is your backbone. When you are going through trials and tribulations of life, your family can be the one that pulls you through as well. When you have God on your side and your family on your side, how can you lose? Amen.

Chapter 29

Everything you do comes back to you

Everything we do comes back to us, good or bad. So whatever we pour into the atmosphere, we will receive it back into our lives, good or bad. That is the way the system works. When the enemy is using us in a negative way, we are responsible for our own actions. Sometimes we can feel in our spirit that we are getting upset. At that moment in time, we have the power to stop and calm ourselves down, and let it go and then.

Sometimes we have the power to engage in negative behavior, and then that is when the enemy is winning. We are responsible for our behavior, our actions. We are responsible for our behavior, good or bad. We are responsible for our character–that is who we are. Whatever you are doing in your life, good or bad, it will come back to you. If you are engaging in positive behavior, then positive behavior will come back to you. If you are engaging in negative behavior then negative behavior will come back to you.

Whatever you engage in, good or bad, you will see it come back to you in your life. If you are doing something negative, being negative, and treating people negatively, then that is what you will receive in your life. If you're being positive, doing positive things, and treating people positively, then you will receive that back in your life.

God bless each and every one of you. You are all in my prayers. God Bless. Love You All.

CHAPTER 30

Family is the key

Family is the backbone of your universe. Family is definitely the key. Amen. When you're going through a situation, family can be right there for you, by your side in a positive way. I know at the beginning of creation, the enemy tried to destroy the family. He tried to break them apart. If you read in the Bible from A to Z, you can see all the destruction that the enemy tries to put upon God's people. You can see now that it is spilling in modern times as well. He is putting a wedge in the middle of families. He has family physically fighting and despising each other, and that's not right.

Family is supposed to be tight. No one should be able to come between family. Amen. The love of a family is awesome. Think back to the incident that drove a wedge between you and your family member. Think hard–is it really worth the rest of your life not speaking to your family member? Can something that serious that could put a wedge between you and your family member for the rest of your life here until you transition into heaven? Think about that.

Take all your problems to God, release them to him on the altar, and leave it there. Amen. Prayer is the key; it truly works. Amen, Brothers and Sisters.

CHAPTER 31

When you both are on the same page in a relationship

When you're both on the same page in a relationship, you both love each other, and you can't live without each other, you always want to be together. When you're both on the same page, that is truly awesome. Amen.

When you are truly committed to each other. Amen. And you won't let the negativity affect your relationship, not one bit, because you know that this person truly loves you, and there's no one on earth like this person. In this world today, there are positive relationships, there are people in relationships, and they are doing the right things. Amen.

God loves us; His love for us is unconditional and timeless. God wants us to love ourselves to the fullest that we possibly can in a positive way. God Bless you all. Stay positive, always stay in a positive frame of mind, always have Jesus Christ on your mind, and always have that mindset to pray, and to pray. Keep God close to your heart. Amen.

CHAPTER 32

Parents

A parent's love for their child is unconditional. From a parent's view, their children can do no wrong and we try to pour positive knowledge into them. Amen. There is nothing we won't do for our children. We pray all the time that they take a positive road in life. We pray all the time that they won't make wrong decisions, that they always make the right ones. We always pray for our children and encourage them as they walk through life. Amen.

There is no love like a parent's love. Amen. A parent will sacrifice their life for their child, and there's nothing that a parent wouldn't do for their children. We are trying to raise our children the best that we possibly can. We love our children, and God knows we do. Amen.

I know that we are on one accord when it comes to our children, and we all pray together in the name of Jesus Christ. Amen. May God Bless us when it comes to our children. May we all be on one accord. Amen.

CHAPTER 33

When someone gives you, their heart

When someone gives you their heart, that is an honor. When someone gives you their heart, you need to respect that. Amen. Cherish it. When someone is giving you their heart, that means something that is something special. They do not want you to break their heart; they want you to cherish their heart because they see something special in you—that's why they chose you.

When someone gives you their heart, they see something special in you. They love you and they are giving a part of themselves to you, so you must treat their heart with love, kindness, happiness, and joy. You must be one with them. It's a big deal. Amen.

When someone is stepping out in faith and giving their heart to you, that is a big deal—something very special. So don't take it lightly. Be respectful of their feelings. Because sometimes it's very hard for someone to open up to someone. Sometimes they think that this person is the one for them.

So when someone is giving you their heart, think about it. Be respectful; don't hurt anyone. Because you don't want anyone to hurt you, always think about someone's feelings, always think about how you would like to be treated,

May God Bless Love You All.

CHAPTER 34

Be very mindful of your surroundings

Always be mindful of your surroundings. Always think before you say something. Always be in a positive frame of mind. And the same way that you believe that God exists, believe that the enemy exists as well. Because he does exist. He is the one they're making it difficult for you. He is the one they're starting trouble for you. He is the one pouring all that drama upon your life.

Always draw from the positive. If something is going wrong in your life, always think. Think about your surroundings, think about what's going on, and make sure that the ways you pray are grounded. Always keep Father God in your heart. You're going to need Him to be your strength. You're going to need Father God will upon your life. Without Him, you will not know how to fight the evil one.

Always pay attention to your surroundings. Yes, God fights your battles, but He needs you to know how to fight the enemy as well. Amen.

May God Bless You All.

CHAPTER 35

When you have a connection with someone

When God has connected you with someone, and you have a connection with them, try to pursue that relationship. Because you feel that connection that God has given to you with this person, and sometimes it's very hard to find people that you are connected with. I am talking about that real connection–you will know when you feel it. God has given us people that we are connected with, and they do exist.

I know some people are saying that love does not exist anymore. Let's talk about love. Let's go to the beginning with the word "love." When you are born your parents pour love into you. They take care of you; they encourage you and pour positivity into you. They teach you how to have manners and what's right or wrong. They do everything that they possibly can do for you in the right way. They try to pour all the right tools into you so you can grow up with all the love that you need in your soul and your spirit in your mind and your wellbeing. They just pour nothing but love into you.

Imagine, as a child growing up, someone not pouring love into you and not being there for you. I remember growing up myself, my mother pouring love into me. Imagine someone growing up without love in their lives, nobody to pour positive into them–all they receive is negativity into their lives. So, they have never experienced love. So, if a person has never had love poured into their lives, and they have never experienced love, so the root of the matter is, how can they love anyone if they have never experienced it?

If they have never experienced love before, then maybe that is some of the reason why they act the way they act in their relationship with people, treating them the way they treat them not in a pleasant way. If you don't have someone to teach you how to love, then how can you truly know what love is and how can you express yourself to someone in a positive way? So, the energy that you give off is negativity, not positive energy because you don't know the foundation of love. That's why you're walking around in a negative way, thinking that your way is okay even when you can't see that you are hurting people.

When people go into a relationship, they go into it in a positive way. They want to have joy and happiness in their lives. They don't want to experience pain in a relationship. You want to be safe in a relationship, and love–that is what people are looking for. Amen.

Your experience of not being loved is affecting other people in a negative way because they are feeding off your negativity in the relationship. Because you are being negative to them, they are feeding off of you, they're feeding off your energy. When you are being negative and mean, you can feel that in your spirit, and you know that you are stepping out of your character. You can feel it. So, try to control yourself.

And if your spirit is so negative, maybe you might need to talk to a minister, a Christian counselor, or somebody that is guided by the Holy Spirit inside of them. Maybe they can pray with you and help you along the way in your journey.

God Bless. Love You All.

CHAPTER 36

Always draw close to your family

Always draw close to your family in any circumstances that you are in. Amen. Family is the key. The love of a family is indescribable. Usually, in certain situations when the enemy has split your family apart, you can feel in the atmosphere that something is missing. Family is very important to your well-being. You can draw from each other in a time of need.

What I mean is when I say that you can draw close to your family members, you can draw from their energy, you can draw from their encouragement. They can pull positive things out of you. You and your family are as one. Amen. A family is beautiful to have, and you will be there for each other, Amen.

Always remember that family is the key. Don't let the enemy tear your family apart. Always keep your family in your prayers. The enemy focuses on every aspect of your life. He focuses on your family as well, trying to tear your family apart. That's what he does. Don't let the enemy win. Always keep your family close to your heart. Amen.

Always keep Father God first in your life. Always keep your family close to your heart. Always pray for your family. Always be in sync with your family. Always pray for your fellow man, and always have your fellow man's back.

And always remember that if you get upset at a moment in time, don't let that moment define you. Continue to keep walking your walk

with God. Pray to God, ask for forgiveness, and move past that moment in time. Don't let that moment define you.

May God Bless You, and God love you all.

CHAPTER 37

God wants you to be whole in every aspect of your life

God wants you to be whole in every aspect of your life. He wants you to be strong in every aspect of your life. He does not want you to have any problems whatsoever in any aspect of your life. God loves togetherness. God does not want you to have any issues in your life.

God wants you to be strong in your personal life; He does not want any issue in that matter. God wants you to be 100% whole in your family life. He doesn't want any issue there as well. Amen. He wants you whole. He really does not want you to experience any drama, but sometimes it slips through, and He's there to catch it and help us along the way. Amen.

Always pray for every aspect of your life so you can be on point. Amen. So, always keep God in the head of your life. Always pray for your well-being, always pray for your family, always pray for your fellow man.

You are better in life with your family than without your family, so if you are having any issue with your family, pray on the matter and try to come back together as one. Don't throw away that family relationship–is very important. God always encourages family. Amen. God Bless.

CHAPTER 38

Be Thankful

When God gives you something in life, be thankful when you receive something in life, be thankful for what you receive in life. Amen. Always have a good heart. Always walk down the positive road in life. Don't let anything negative affect you in life. Always stay positive and focus on the good.

If something negative happens to you in life, turn it around and make it into something positive. Amen.

In a relationship in life, always be truthful and always be honest. Once you're not honest in a relationship, you're opening the door for negativity to walk in and affect your relationship in a negative way. You always want your relationship to be in the positive realm. You always want God to cover your relationship in a positive way. Amen.

Because once you open the door for negativity in your relationship, everything goes wrong. So always stay in the positive realm, and your relationship will remain perfect in every way in your life. Amen. God Bless.

CHAPTER 39

God will give you true love.

Love is real God will give you true love Amen. Yes, he will there's someone for everyone true love does exist God wants us all to be happy. Amen.

The enemy does not want you happy, so he will do all he can do to bring destruction into your life. Amen. He likes to destroy your relationships. In a relationship, you're going to have good days and you're going to have bad days. Keep pressing through, give your relationship to God, and pray for your relationship. God is the key to your solution.

If your relationship is something that you can handle, that's fine and dandy. Fight for it. But if your relationship is over the top, and your spouse is mentally and physically abusing you, then you need to think about that twice. You need to get help in the natural and in the spirit realm. God didn't intend for us to be in any bad relationship. God wants nothing but joy and happiness in our lives. That's what he wants to pour on us on a day-to-day basis.

God Bless Love you all. Stay positive.

CHAPTER 40

Pray for your family and your fellowman

Always pray for your family. Family is the key. Always lend a helping hand to your fellow man and always keep them in your prayers as well. Amen. Family is the key God desires. The enemy does not desire family. He is on the rampage, destroying family lives. He is manipulating the situation so people cannot really see what's going on. So many families are broken apart due to the negative influence of the enemy. Yes, it's the truth. The enemy is pouring all this negativity upon the earth, destroying family members' relationships.

It is not natural for families to fight each other on a day-to-day basis. Sometimes you might get into a little tiff with one of your family members, but then you apologize, and everything is alright. It is not natural for you to get into a blow-out fight with your family member for years, not talk to them, and you have a hatred towards them. Right here, you can see very clearly that the enemy is influencing that behavior. Because we were designed to love our family to be one with our family.

Think about it. Does that sound normal for someone to hate their family member? God loves us all. God wants us all to be on one accord, fighting a good fight of faith. God does not want us on one accord fighting our family. The enemy is behind all the negativity that's in this earth today.

Please always focus on your family in a positive way. Always pray for them and always have good energy towards them. Because there is nothing like your family. Always pray for your fellow man. Amen.

May God Bless You.

CHAPTER 41

When it comes to your relationships God is on your side in a positive way

When it comes to your relationships, God is on your side in a positive way. He will fight for you in every aspect of your life. Stay positive, always have God in your heart. Always pray for your family and for your fellowmen.

In any aspect of your life, God is on your side; He wants you to win in life. Amen. In your family life, he wants you to be strong and in your dating life, He wants you stronger as well. He wants you to be very happy in life. Yes, He does. Amen.

Always stay positive and always focus on the good. God is good and He will make your life bright for you. Amen. When you choose God in life, he will shield you from all the negativity that comes upon you. He will definitely fight your battles for you. Amen. May God Bless You All.

CHAPTER 42

The person God has for you is out there

Sometimes in life, you are trying to find a companion. You are not very successful in that matter, Amen. The person God has for you is out there waiting on you. God waits patiently for you. Yes, he does.

At that moment in time when God thinks that you are ready to receive love in your life, He's right there on time. You can find love walking down the street, minding your own business; you can find love anywhere. A family member can introduce you to someone, and you can find love when God is ready for you to receive love in your life. He will give it to you. Amen.

So, don't give up on love, it does exist. It's waiting for you patiently. God has your back in life. Yes, he does. So always pray, always keep God strong in your heart, always pray for your family, always pray for your fellowmen. God has your back; true love does exist. Pray on it and keep walking by faith. Amen. May God Bless You and Love You All.

CHAPTER 43

Stand on the word of God, He hears you

Stand on the word of God, for He hears you and he will be right there on time for you. Amen. He will never leave you; He is always there for you. If you ask him for something, pray for that matter, stand right there in faith on that matter and don't leave that matter he will be there for you. Amen.

If you have made a prayer request to God, you stand strong in faith on that matter. He hears you. Sometimes, He may not answer you when you want, but he is right on time. So, continue to pray and pray. God is here for you. Amen. He is nothing but love.

Always keep Him strong in your heart. Always walk by faith and try to do the right things. Let God guide you; let God show you the right way to live. Amen. God loves you, and there is nothing on earth that he will not do for you, my brothers and my sisters. May God Bless You All.

CHAPTER 44

You should be praying about everything in your life

You should be praying about everything in your life 100% every single day, with the enemy running rapidly in the world today, Amen. God loves us dearly. He wants us to be 100% healed and whole in every aspect of our lives. Yes, he does.

So, don't let the enemy distract you in any means necessary. Amen. Always focus on your surroundings, always know what's going on, and always pay close attention to your surroundings at all times. Always stay connected to Father God because you are going to need Father God to help along the way.

So, always have that mindset to keep God on your mind. Pray like you never prayed before and always walk around in good spirits. Amen. Sometimes, it's nice that you can get your friends together, and all of you can pray together. There is power in numbers. Amen. God Bless.

So, always keep Father God strong in your heart, soul, spirit and your mind. May God Bless you, and God Love You All.

CHAPTER 45

Finding true love and holding on to it

Finding true love and holding onto it. Love is a blessing. People are thirsting for real love today. Some people say real love does not exist today. So, if you find it, hold on to it and never let it go.

Because you are opening up yourself to someone, and sometimes people are not being truthful with you. Sometimes people are not on the same wavelength as you are; their motives are not the same motives as yours.

Make sure before you step into the dating scene, make sure your mind and spirit are 100% clear so you can spot the right person. You don't want any drama in your life; you want to be with the right person. God wants you to be happy, not sad. You want joy in your life, nothing but joy Amen.

Always pray to Father God before you make any decision. Always ask for His advice before you step out and do anything in life. Amen. God Bless Stay Positive. True Love Does Exist. Wait patiently for it. Amen. God Love You All.

CHAPTER 46

God wants us to always be praying

God wants us to always have a praying mindset. Amen. God wants us to always be praying, so always have that mindset to have God on your mind.

Before you go to bed at night, get on your hands and knees and pray. When you wake up in the morning, get on your hands and knees and pray. Pray throughout the day; just take a moment and pray. Just have that mindset to have Jesus Christ on your mind every single day. Amen.

You might have good days or bad days but keep pushing through. God loves you; He is on your side, and he wants you to achieve in every aspect of your life. Amen.

So, always stay focused, always pray and always have that mindset to have Jesus Christ in your mind. Because in times of need, you're going to need the Lord himself to pull you through anything that you go through in the world today. Amen.

May God Bless You and God Love You All.

CHAPTER 47

Grandparents

Grandparents are truly blessed. They get a chance to bite at the apple twice. What I mean is, sometimes in life, we feel that with our own children we made mistakes, and we wish we had not done it this way. But when God blesses us with grandchildren, we feel that God has given us a second chance, and we can make it right through our grandchildren. Amen.

With our relationship with our grandchildren, our grandchildren look up to us. We have an obligation to our grandchildren to be the best grandparents that we can possibly be in life. Amen. So, always let your grandchildren see you in a positive light. In a time of need, always be there for your grandchildren. They are counting on you. In any circumstances in life, they need you to be there for them.

Sometimes their parents might need you to step in along the way to help them out. Like I said, being a grandparent is a blessing. May God Bless You, and God Love You All.

CHAPTER 48

Stay positive

Always stay in the positive realm of life. Always know what's right and what's wrong, and always do the right thing. Don't let anyone influence you into doing anything that's wrong.

Always have good intentions. Always stay in a positive frame of mind. Always pray and ask God for His advice. Always put God at the top of your life. If you stay positive, focus on the positive and block out the negativity that's around you, then you should be fine.

Don't let negativity bring you down in life. Amen. You want to win in life; you want to do the best that you possibly can in life. So, focus on the positive, be the best you that you possibly can, and walk down a righteous path in life. God has your back. He loves you.

May God Bless You and God love you All. Amen.

CHAPTER 49

Waiting patiently for God

Waiting patiently for God. You have called on the Lord, and you do not see results immediately. He hears you. Stand on the word of God and doesn't move from that moment that you pray to him. He hears you. He's there for you–just have patience. Amen.

Sometimes, we feel that God does not hear us, or He does hear us, and he is ignoring our cries for help. Amen. Sometimes, we feel that we are in dire need, and that He needs to immediately answer us. This is how we feel sometimes–that God is ignoring us and does not want to help us. We get frustrated sometimes, not hearing from God, not understanding why he is not listening to us.

Don't feel that way. He is there. He understands our situation. He is in the mix of the circumstances, fixing it for us Amen. So don't think that God is not there for you when you pray, and your prayers are not answered immediately. He is behind the scenes, orchestrating something great for you. He is fixing the problem that you prayed for.

He does not want you to suffer in life; He wants you to walk down the right path in life. He is making sure that you have a perfect life. So, always know that God is there for you. Sometimes it may seem that he is dragging His feet when it comes to you but He's not, he's just a patient.

May God Bless You, and may God love you all.

CHAPTER 50

Children

As children, we love our parents. We look up to our parents, and we take our directions from our parents. As we grow up, sometimes we mimic what our parents do in life. Amen.

When we're going through something, your parents are always there to give their advice and give their helping hand as well. Amen. As children, we try to do our very best in life so our parents can be very proud of us. We take their advice, and we use it in a positive way to walk down the right road in life. Amen.

We take what our parents say very seriously. We love them dearly, yes, we do. We are a blessing from God and from our parents. God and our parents want us to live our life to the fullest that we possibly can. They want us to win in life. They want us to be winners. Amen.

Stay positive, stay in a positive state of mind.

May God Bless You and God Love You.

CHAPTER 51

Keep your mind clear

Keep your mind clear at all times. Don't let any fear get in your spirit. If you pray to God for something and you believe in your heart that it will come to a pass, then it is done. Because what you believe in your heart will come to you. Amen.

Thank you in Jesus' name. Keep your heart and spirit clear at all times. Stay focused on God. God is a miracle worker, yes, He is. You can focus better when your heart is clear and your spirit is as well. Amen. So, always keep a clear mind. Don't let negativity bring you down; always focus on the positive. Amen.

Don't let fear control you. You have the power to stand strong in faith. Faith is the key–the faith that can move mountains. All you have to do is believe, and you will receive whatever you want in life. Amen.

May God Bless You and Stay Positive.

CHAPTER 52

Always pray for the other person in your life

If you have someone in your life and they are very important to you, you make sure that you pray for them and you make sure that you keep them in your prayers. You make sure that you keep sending their name up to God because you want them to be covered at all times. You want God smiling down on them at all times. Amen.

God is love, and you want God's love to protect them at all times. You want God's presence to be very strong in their lives. Prayer is the key. Always pray for the other person in your life. Prayer moves mountains if you want it to. You have to believe that you will receive Jesus Christ in your life, and everything will fall into places for you.

Always try to be the best you that you possibly can be. Amen.

CHAPTER 53

After you pray, always listen to God's advice

When you pray to God, after you're done praying, then listen deep within your spirit. Because God will start talking to your spirit after you pray, that's when He will start communicating with you. He will let you know what He wants you to do or letting you know what's going to happen. God does answer prayers. Sometimes the prayer that we ask Him for he might not give it to us right then and there; it's a whole process going on. But He is right on time, and he will never forsake us. So, don't ever stop praying to God; He is your only answer. Amen.

He is our only God, and He knows what's right and wrong for us. Sometimes we can't see the whole picture, but He can. Amen. So, never give up on yourself, never give up on God. Because God is always there for you. Sometimes you might see something the way you see it, and it's not really the way it is. God knows the real way. So always believe in God and leave your burden at God's door.

May God Bless You and God Love You All.

CHAPTER 54

You always want your relationship to be in God's hands

You always want your relationship to be in God's hands. Yes, we do. You want your relationship blessed; you want your relationship to be in God's hands so He can cover you at all times. Amen.

God is love, and you want your relationship to experience love–real love, agape love, the love how God loves us. That eternal love. Sometimes in life, if you have been wounded in a relationship, make sure you get yourself together and get your thinking process correct before you step out into another relationship. Ensure that God controls that relationship and makes sure you get your advice from God. He is the only one that knows the future; He's the only one that knows what's going on.

Your help comes from the Lord. Amen. So always pray, always keep your spirit in tune are in line with God, and always tries to have peace of mind.

May God Bless You.

CHAPTER 55

Love God with your whole heart, your soul, your spirit, and your mind

Always love God with your whole heart, your soul, your spirit, and your mind. Always put the focus on God. Always focus on God. Your heart, your soul, your spirit, and your mind are all intertwined together as one; they feed off of each other. They can't work without one another.

Your spirit is intertwined together as one; it works with your heart, with your soul, and your mind. Your spirit possesses your whole body in return for you. Your spirit is connected to who you are, your wellbeing. Your spirit is the connection to God. God is spirit, so His spirit can communicate with your spirit.

So always focus on God throughout the whole day and make Him your number one priority. Amen. He is your help. Your help comes from God. So always have a love for God in your heart, your soul, your spirit, and your mind. May God Bless You.

CHAPTER 56

Brothers and Sisters

I do not have any brothers or sisters. I am the only child that my parents have. My view on brothers and sisters is by watching my children interact with each other and observing other brothers and sisters. This is what I have learned; the love that they have for each other is priceless, and they would do anything for each other.

When my children were growing up, I cannot remember them fighting–maybe a little disagreement somewhere, but nothing serious. My children are adults now, and the love that they have for each other is still embedded deep down inside of them for each other. I am so glad that God has His hands on my children's lives and on other brothers' and sisters' lives as well.

One thing about God when he puts His hands on you, He puts his hands on you for dear life. Amen. There's nothing like the spirit of the Lord running through you; there's no feeling like it on earth, the Holy Spirit. Amen. Can dwell in you if you want it to. Brother and sister appreciate each other. God made you brothers and sisters for a reason to love each other and respect each other. I know sometimes siblings don't get along. But you can overcome all that negative that's surrounding you in the world today and have a positive relationship with your siblings. I am praying that all the brothers and sisters today get on one accord and fight a good fight of faith for their relationship with their siblings if you have a terrific relationship with your siblings then I'm not talking to you God bless you I am talking to the siblings that are struggling in that area you're in my prayers and I'm praying every day for you to wake-up and have a terrific relationship with your siblings Amen. May God Bless You.

CHAPTER 57

Be Grateful

When you receive something positive in your life, be grateful for what God has done for you. Sometimes we get caught up in ourselves and we can't really see what's going on around us. Sometimes we are caught up in foolishness. We are supposed to be doing one thing, but we will focus on something else, acting like it's all about us. It's not all about us; it's all about us getting our act together bringing God into our lives.

We need to stand up strong and tall and help the human race. That's what it's all about–God's word getting out, and that's what it's all about–helping people. Amen. The way God loves us, He wants us to love our fellow men the same way. So always have a kind spirit, always be grateful for what God has done for you,

Always be grateful when someone does something for you. Always tell them "Thank you" to let them know that you care about what they have done for you. Amen.

May God Bless You.

CHAPTER 58

Be hopeful

Be hopeful. I know sometimes you're in a certain situation and you're praying to God for to help, asking Him to get you out of that situation. And you see there's no God anywhere in sight, and you are losing hope. Be hopeful.

Sometimes it looks like God is not there, but He is there, and He is designing something for you to come out of that situation on top. He never wants you to lose in life. He always wants you to win in life. He is very proud of us; and his will is for us to always be winners. That's His will for us. He is a wonderful Father, so always be hopeful.

If you are in a situation and it looks like God is not answering your prayers, just take a step back, think, and pray and say God always wants me to win in life he does hear me and He is right on time. Amen.

May God Bless You.

CHAPTER 59

Never give up on love

If you have gone through some trauma in your relationship and it ended badly, don't use that as an excuse to not find true love. Never give up on love. Take your time first and find out who you really are. Don't rush; get your mind clear and focused.

After trauma, usually people want to be alone, and they are very vulnerable and can be easily persuaded. So that's why you should relax. You shouldn't think about getting right into a relationship right after you just went through some serious trauma in your relationship.

After the incident, take a look back at your life and focus on your life. Focus on how you got here. First, pray to God and ask God to help you. Ask God how you arrived here. Focus on what He is telling you. Because sometimes we do not give ourselves any chance to heal from the trauma we went through from our past relationship. We jump right into a new relationship with that old trauma without giving us a chance to heal. We need to heal so we can go into a healthy relationship.

If you do not get the proper treatment, you will walk down the wrong road in relationships because of your trauma. The root of the matter is that you just got out of a bad relationship, so you are feeling bad about yourself because the relationship didn't survive. You went through some trauma, and now you have to get your head on straight.

Sometimes we don't heal, and we jump right into a new relationship right after we just came out of a messy relationship. That's not good. We need time to heal and think. Just focus on yourself, focus on who

you really are. You just got out of this relationship with this person you probably thought you were going to be with forever, and that moment in time has shaken the core of your universe. Now you don't know what to do.

If you have tried to get yourself together and it seems like you are not getting back to yourself, it's alright to reach out for help. It's alright to seek guidance in this matter so you can be 100% healed. Because God wants you to be happy. God wants you to experience so much joy in your life. The right person is out there waiting for you. All you have to do is get yourself mentally and physically together, and then God will tell you when it's time for you to go back out there. Because you might get yourself caught up in a situation that you don't want to be in.

Stay calm, stay focused, pray to God, and God has the answers that you are looking for. May God bless you and God love you all.

CHAPTER 60

Worship God in Prayers and in Spirit

Worship God in prayers and in spirit. As you worship the Lord, you can feel His presence as you go into deep, deep worship. You are getting a strong connection with God. Sometimes He pulls you into one of His realms with Him. You can feel the glory of the Lord all around you as you worship Him. The power of the Lord can be very intense as you worship the Lord. We give Him all the praise.

Yes, worship is definitely the key. Amen. When you are praying and worshiping the Lord, you are rising up so high in His presence. Amen. We truly love the Lord. There is nothing on earth that we would not do to keep this deep connection with the Lord. So always worship the Lord; He is worthy to be praised. Always pray; our help comes from the Lord. Amen.

May God bless you and stay positive

CHAPTER 61

Jesus will always be by your side

When you accept Jesus Christ in your life, He will always be by your side. He will never ever forsake you. Amen. He is a miracle worker, yes, He is. When He is on your side, you can't lose in life. Turn your life over to God, and you will have a winning hand in life.

You might still have a little bump in the road through life, but it's better to have God by your side as you transition through your everyday life. Everything will change for the better for you once you receive Jesus Christ in your life.

Always have that giving spirit, always have that spirit to do what's right. Always pour positivity into the atmosphere. Never pour negativity into the atmosphere. Remember, what you pour into the atmosphere, good or bad, you will receive it back in your life.

May God bless you and God loves you all. Jesus will always be by your side. Amen.

CHAPTER 62

The main source of our relationship failing is the enemy.

The main source of our relationship failing is the enemy. The enemy's plan is to destroy your happiness. He does not want you to experience any happiness or joy. When the enemy sees that you are happy in your relationship, that's when he throws chaos and confusion at you.

We are responsible for our well-being. We are responsible for our conduct. We are responsible for the way we live our lives. We are very aware of the enemy's behavior. He is the negative force that surrounds us. He is always somewhere pulling negativity out of someone. If someone is acting badly, he has something to do with it. We should not allow the enemy to destroy our happiness.

If you are in a relationship with someone and you are being inappropriate, think for a minute: am I being influenced by God or am I being influenced by the enemy? Think about that for a moment, because your behavior will let you know who you are being influenced by.

We should stand up and take responsibility for our actions. We should not allow the enemy to use us for his bidding. We should not allow the enemy to use us so we can hurt people. Stand up, do what you need to do, take the appropriate steps so you can stop the enemy from using you for his bidding. You know what you need to do to stop it.

May God bless you and God love you all.

CHAPTER 63

Grandchildren

As grandchildren, we look up to our grandparents. We love them dearly and we respect them. Amen. We cherish them and we know in our hearts our grandparents would do anything for us.

As grandchildren, we get to live in two worlds. We get to experience the love of our grandparents. It's like different avenues, but it's our parents and our grandparents pouring love into our lives. Knowledge, paving the way for us to have a better life, doing all they can so we can achieve all our goals in life. Amen.

We look up to our elders, the ones that pave the way for us. May God bless you.

CHAPTER 64

Uncle and Auntie

Uncles and aunties are beautiful to have in your life, and they are a blessing as well. Because they get a chance sometimes to experience that connection with children before they receive their own children sometimes.

I am an only child, so growing up, I was raised around my aunt. She was like a sister to me. She was one year older than I was, and we did sister things together. She is my mother's sister. Through that relationship with her, I got to experience how it felt to have a sister.

Uncles and aunts play a big role in our lives. They are there for us, and when we ask them for something in our time of need, they will be there for us. We are truly blessed. Thank you, Father God, for blessing us with our uncles and our aunties in the world today.

May God bless you.

CHAPTER 65

When you say something negative about your spouse to someone, you have crossed the line.

If you are engaging in a negative conversation about your spouse to someone, you have crossed the line. That's not God's will for you to do that. If you and your spouse had a misunderstanding and you cannot get on the same page with him or her, maybe you could go speak to someone about the matter. Because a married couple is twining together as one, God has placed them together in one realm. It's a physical and spiritual connection between them. God does not want any outsiders to come into their realm.

A spouse should not be engaging in any negative behavior about their spouse, and they should not be listening to anyone that says anything negative about their spouse to them. You have to think deep down in your spirit: what kind of person would allow someone to stand there and say something negative about their spouse to you? Remember, God has brought you and this person together, supposed to be forever. Sometimes the enemy can see that you're doing excellent over there in your realm, and he throws a lot of daggers. You got to pay attention to that.

Always pray for every aspect of your life, and if you think you need to talk to someone about your marriage, there's nothing wrong with that if you need guidance to help you along the way.

May God bless you and God love you all.

CHAPTER 66

God's heart desires for you

God's heart desire for you is to live your life to the fullest that you possibly can. He wants all your dreams to come true. There's nothing on earth that He will not do for you. God wants you to be in tune with Him. God wants to have a deep relationship with you. God wants you to have a strong prayer life with Him.

We should remember that God is the one that created us. We should remember that God should come first in our lives, not secondary in our life. In the morning when we wake up, before we put our foot on the floor, we should thank God for that breath that we are about to take. Sometimes we forget that God plays a big role in our lives. We have to remember how we came to be.

May God bless you.

INSPIRATIONAL MESSAGE

My view on relationships is that in the beginning, God's purpose was for us to live in harmony. Our problem was when the enemy deceived Eve. He poured negativity into the atmosphere. That opened the door for us to feed off of it. The negativity is what he feeds off of. Right from the beginning, his target was to bring us down. He used Eve to bring us down, and now we are paying for that moment in time.

I believe that that's why we have problems with relationships. He sees you are in a relationship and he sees that you are happy. The key is happiness. That's when he focuses on you. His motive is to attack every aspect of your life. He pulls negativity into the atmosphere. He has couples fighting each other, mothers fighting fathers, brothers and sisters fighting, uncles and aunties fighting. He has a whole lot of people fighting each other.

We should stop fighting each other and focus on what's the real problem. What's really happening here? The enemy is turning us all against each other. We need to focus on that; that is the real problem. We need to rise up together in one accord and fight the good fight of faith. The enemy is the problem, not your fellow men.

May God bless you all. You are all in my prayers. Remain faithful to God who is always there for you. Always pray, always have that mindset to have Father God on your mind 24 hours a day. And we are going to fight for our happiness. The enemy is not going to take that from us. We have to have accountability for our actions. We have to stop doing that. Allow the enemy to use us in a negative way. We have to be responsible for our own actions. Amen.

May God bless you all and God loves you all.

www.ingramcontent.com/pod-product-compliance
Lightning Source LLC
Chambersburg PA
CBHW051230120626

46547CB00013B/1580